UNCOVERING HISTORY

THE VIKINGS

First published by McRae Books
Copyright © 2003 McRae Books Srl, Florence (Italy)
Borgo Santa Croce, 8 – 50122 – Florence (Italy)
This edition published under license from McRae Books. All rights
reserved.

SERIES EDITOR Anne McRae
TEXT Neil Grant
CONSULTANT Caroline Paterson
ART CONSULTANT Andrea Ricciardi di Gaudesi
ILLUSTRATIONS Manuela Cappon, Lorenzo Cecchi, Valeria Ferretti,
Giacinto Gaudenzi, Alessandro Menchi, Antonella Pastorelli, Paola
Ravaglia, Claudia Saraceni, Giacomo Soriani, Studio Stalio (Alessandro
Cantucci, Fabiano Fabbrucci, Andrea Morandi)
GRAPHIC DESIGN Marco Nardi
LAYOUT Nick Leggett, Starrydog Books
EDITING Claire Moore and Anne McRae
REPRO Litocolor, Florence
PICTURE RESEARCH Claire Moore

Published in the United States by Smart Apple Media
2140 Howard Drive West, North Mankato, Minnesota 56003

U.S. publication copyright © 2006 Smart Apple Media
International copyright reserved in all countries. No part of this book
may be reproduced in any form without written permission from the
publisher.
Printed and bound in Belgium

Library of Congress Cataloging-in-Publication Data

Grant, Neil, 1938-
Everyday life of the vikings / by Neil Grant.
p. cm. — (Uncovering history)
Includes index.
ISBN 1-58340-706-5
1. Vikings—Juvenile literature. 2. Civilization, Viking—Juvenile literature.
I. Title. II. Series.

DL65.G65 2005
948'.022—dc22   2004051210

9 8 7 6 5 4 3 2 1

UNCOVERING HISTORY

Neil Grant

EVERYDAY LIFE OF THE

VIKINGS

Illustrations by Manuela Cappon, Lorenzo Cecchi, Valeria Ferretti, Giacinto Gaudenzi, Alessandro Menchi, Antonella Pastorelli, Paola Ravaglia, Claudia Saraceni, Giacomo Soriani, Studio Stalio (Alessandro Cantucci, Fabiano Fabbrucci, Andrea Morandi)

A⁺
Smart Apple Media

Contents

Introduction

About 1,000 years ago, the Vikings were the most powerful people in Europe. Their homeland was Scandinavia in northwest Europe, which consists of modern-day Denmark, Sweden, and Norway. They spoke Old Norse, the language from which Danish, Swedish, and Norwegian developed. During the Viking age, which lasted from the late 8th century to the late 11th century, the Scandinavians became Christians, and the rule of kings was established.

It was a time of great drama. To the neighboring peoples of Christian Europe, the Vikings seemed like terrifying pagans who raided their countries, carrying off people and treasure. But they were not only pirates. Like their Christian neighbors, the Vikings were farmers, fishermen, and craftsmen. Expert sailors, they became great travelers and explorers, settling in Iceland and Greenland and traveling across Russia as far as Turkey and Iran. Many settled peacefully in other countries.

Since the Vikings did not keep written records until later times, we know about how they lived mainly from the writings of others and from the discoveries of archaeologists. We still do not fully understand the reasons for the great expansion that carried them across nearly half the world, from the fringes of North America to the fringes of Asia. Possible reasons were the need for more land, the fierce wars between rival chiefs, and a powerful spirit of adventure.

Chronology of The Vikings

VIKINGS RAID THE ENGLISH MONASTERY OF LINDISFARNE 793

VIKINGS SETTLE IN DUBLIN
841

FIRST RAIDS ON PARIS AND HAMBURG
845

VIKINGS IN THE MEDITERRANEAN
c. 860

NOVGOROD BECOMES CAPITAL OF RUS
c. 860

VIKING SETTLERS IN FAROES AND ICELAND
860–900

HAROLD FINEHAIR ESTABLISHES EARLDOM OF ORKNEY
c. 874

KING ALFRED DIVIDES ENGLAND WITH DANISH LEADER GUTHRUM
878

ROLLO'S BAND SETTLES IN NORMANDY
911

VIKINGS IN THE CASPIAN SEA
912

VARANGIAN GUARD FOUNDED IN CONSTANTINOPLE
c. 980

ERIC THE RED SETTLES IN GREENLAND
c. 985

OLAF TRYGGVASON UNITES NORWAY
995

LEIF ERICSSON DISCOVERS NORTH AMERICA
c. 1000

DUBLIN NORSEMEN DEFEATED BY IRISH KING BRIAN BORU AT CLONTARF
1014

DANISH KING CNUT RULES ENGLAND
1016–35

DEFEAT OF NORWEGIAN KING HAROLD HARDRADA'S INVASION OF ENGLAND
1066

Viking Origins

Above: This typical bronze, silver, and gold brooch shows that Gotland was rich. Such brooches have only been found on Gotland.

The people we call Vikings lived in Scandinavia (Denmark, Sweden, and Norway) and spoke Old Norse (the ancestral language of Danish, Swedish, and Norwegian). Historians date the Viking age from about 793 to 1066, but these dates are just markers. The name "Viking" probably comes from a word meaning pirate, or bandit, describing those who raided nearby European countries. Raiding was part of the great Viking expansion, as they spread to other countries in Europe and the North Atlantic. However, not all Vikings were raiders. Vikings, also called "Norsemen" or "Northmen," were traders and settlers as well.

Below: A settlement in Viking Norway. The mountains protected farm land and sheltered the fjords—valleys flooded by the sea—from gales, so travel by water was much easier than travel by land.

The Viking homelands

Scandinavia covers a huge area and is more than six times the size of New York. Landscape and climate vary greatly, and many regions were uninhabited. Since Scandinavia has a long coastline (Norway's alone is more than 12,400 miles, or 20,000 km, long) and many islands, the Vikings were sea people. Although parts of Scandinavia are above the Arctic Circle, the warming effect of the Gulf Stream keeps the climate warmer than might be expected.

A silver pendant of a warrior's head found in southeast Sweden.

Most of Norway and Sweden were covered by mountains or forests, and most people lived near the sea. Viking Denmark (which included some of southern Sweden and northern Germany) was flat, with more farm land.

The early Scandinavians

At the end of the Ice Age (10,000 years ago), the first human beings began moving into the Scandinavian country of Denmark. They were probably the direct ancestors of the Vikings, since Scandinavia had no great waves of immigrants from other lands.

The Viking people

The best evidence of the Viking people comes from their graves. They were slightly shorter than people in modern-day Scandinavia. Many people lived to be 40 or 50 years old, which was a good life span at that time. They had good teeth, since they ate only a little bit of sugar. Due to hard physical work and a cold climate, however, they often suffered from arthritis. Although distinct from other Europeans (especially in religion), their way of life was not very different from neighboring peoples.

The ancestors of the Vikings sacrificed humans to their gods. They threw the bodies into bogs, where some were preserved. Above: Tollund man, now in a Danish museum, was sacrificed.

The Viking expansion

No one knows for certain why so many people left their homeland during the Viking age. One likely reason is that the population had grown so fast that good land was becoming scarce. If only one son was to inherit the family farm, his brothers had to either emigrate or make a living from raiding and piracy.

Whether they were Viking raiders, traders, or emigrants, knowledge of ships and the sea helped them in their travels.

Viking Society

Scandinavia was never part of the ancient Roman world, so it did not experience central government, written laws, or Christianity. There were no real towns. People lived in small farming settlements led by a chief, who owned the most land. By the beginning of the Viking age, a small number of families were gaining control, especially in Denmark, where the country was less rugged and easier to manage. The local ruler was war chief as well as governor. Only Denmark had a king before 900, but by the 11th century, all of the Scandinavian countries were monarchies.

Most slaves were captured in Viking raids. They were at the bottom of Viking society, after the king or chief, nobles, and freemen.

Viking law

Few people could read or write, and Viking law was made up of the customs of the people and the judgments of the leading men, which were reached by general agreement. The first written code of laws, the "Jonsbok," was recorded in Iceland about 200 years after the end of the Viking age.

From kings to slaves

From evidence found in graves, it appears that Viking people were divided into several distinct social classes. At the top was the chief or king. Below him came his warrior-nobles, or earls (jarls). Next came the ordinary freemen, farmers, and traders (karls), who also fought if needed. At the bottom came the slaves (thralls).

One sign of a king's authority was the issue of coins. These silver coins (above) are from about 1000 and bear the name and portrait of the Danish king Svein Forkbeard.

A page from an early copy of the "Jonsbok," which dates from a time after the Vikings had become Christians.

Crime and punishment

Life was cheap and often violent. Feuds and murders were so common that they were sometimes settled by paying compensation to the dead man's family or sending the killer into exile. Judgments were made in the Thing or through trial by ordeal, which might include picking up red-hot metal (if the wound healed well, the accused person was innocent).

This man has been hanged for stealing sheep, a crime sometimes treated as more serious than murder. Penalties often depended on the importance of the accused person.

Women

Men were powerful, but women were also very important in Viking society. Marriage was an equal partnership. The woman looked after the children and household business. Women did not fight or hunt, and, with rare exceptions, they were not traders or professional craft workers, but they did run the farm when the men were away on raids. Women of high status could be very influential—the richest Viking grave ever found was a woman's.

Left: Woman as peacekeeper. In this carving, a woman holds back a man, perhaps her husband, who is about to attack a mounted hunter with a knife.

The Thing

The Thing was a local assembly of freemen that met once a year or more. It made laws and acted as a court to settle quarrels between individuals and pass judgment on crimes such as murder and theft. Decisions were reached by casting lots. The Thing was also a place where people exchanged gossip, arranged marriages, or made business deals. Freemen met in a special place in the open, usually a low hill or mound (such as the Tynwald on the Isle of Man) surrounded by low ground. The Thing was an important institution to the Vikings and existed wherever they settled. As kings gained control, however, the Thing gradually lost its power.

Men arriving for a meeting of the Thing. All freemen were expected to attend, and each man had the right to speak.

The Althing met at Thingvellir, 30 miles (50 km) east of Reykjavik in Iceland. A natural wall of volcanic lava made a good sounding board for speakers' voices. The Law-Speaker presided from Law Rock.

The Althing

Iceland had no king until Norway took over in 1262. The government belonged to a national assembly, the Althing, often called the world's first parliament. It met for two weeks every summer under an elected president, the Law-Speaker, and included men from all local assemblies (some traveled 17 days to get there). With no police force, the Althing's authority depended on the people's desire for law and order.

Overland Travel

From Arctic Norway to temperate Denmark, Scandinavia covers nearly 309,000 square miles (800,000 sq km). The land and climate of this huge region vary greatly. Norway and parts of Sweden are mountainous. Forests cover large areas, and good farming soil is scarce. Winters are long and cold, especially in the north and east. More people lived in mild, fertile Denmark than in harsh, rugged Norway, although Norway is eight times larger. People traveled overland on foot, by wagon, or on horseback but went by water if they could, since it was safer and quicker. Overland travel from Skåne to Uppland took a month; by sea, it took five days.

This reconstructed ninth-century tapestry shows people on foot, on horseback, and in wagons.

Roads

No roads as we know them existed. Instead, most roads were unsurfaced tracks. The Vikings laid down branches in marshy areas, and in well-traveled places, they built both wooden tracks and stone pavements for carts. Traces of the Army Road, which ran nearly 190 miles (300 km) through Jutland, can still be seen today. Crossroads and important junctions were often marked by a rune stone, or carved monument. The Vikings seldom built bridges, preferring to cross rivers at fords or by ferry.

A 10th-century silver figure of a warrior on his horse. It was found at Birka in Sweden.

Carts and wagons

Simple wooden carts and wagons drawn by horses were used on farms and to carry goods from place to place. Their use was restricted by weather conditions, and in wet weather, their wheels made big ruts in the track.

Carts often had a removable body. In winter, the body could be taken off the wheels and put on a sled. Like ships, cart bodies were sometimes used for burials.

A winter scene in Viking Scandinavia. On the left, a horse pulls a litter, loaded with stores, on runners.

The single skis used by this man and woman are from later times and were probably used by the Vikings, too.

The Vikings used wooden skis and skates made of animal bone, which were strapped to the foot. They resembled short skis, with a broad edge. The skater pushed himself along with spiked sticks.

This beautifully carved sled was found in the Oseberg ship burial. Wooden sleds were important for winter transportation.

Winter travel

In many parts of Scandinavia, traveling overland was much easier in the winter than in the summer. In cold weather, marshy ground was frozen, as were lakes and some rivers. When making a journey on foot, skates and skis, made of pinewood and up to six feet (2 m) long, were a big help. Horses were fitted with crampons (small iron plates with spikes) and could pull a heavily loaded sled over the snow more easily than they could pull a wheeled cart along muddy, rutted tracks.

Shipbuilding

The importance of ships to the Vikings is shown by their use in religious ceremonies. The Vikings were the best seamen in Europe, and they built the finest ships. Best-known are their longships—long, narrow warships with a shallow frame that enabled them to sail in shallow waters. They could reach 10 knots (12 miles, or 20 km, per hour). Such seagoing vessels had a single, rectangular sail, probably made of strips of woolen cloth sewn together. The sail carried them across the open sea, but oars allowed them to maneuver in coastal waters and rivers.

Above: The ship was steered by an extra-large oar on the right (starboard) side of the stern.

Elaborate dragon heads were often made for ships. Dragon heads, a favorite subject of Viking craftsmen, appear in many places.

Viking traders in Russia traveled by river. When they had to move around obstacles or change rivers, they carried their boat over the land with everything in it.

Viking ships

Besides their longships, the Vikings built many other types of vessels. Cargo ships, and those that carried emigrants across the Atlantic, were broader and deeper. Other types of ships included flat-bottomed ferries and small rowboats for local journeys. To visit friends in a neighboring valley, it was often easiest to sail down to the sea and up the next river.

Decoration

The high prow allowed the Vikings to decorate their ships with patterns or figureheads, especially dragons' heads. Carved by specialist craftsmen, they were perhaps meant to protect the ship or frighten enemies. An Icelandic legend says that dragon heads should be removed when approaching a friendly shore, in case they upset the local spirits.

A busy scene in a Viking shipyard. The secret to the strength of Viking ships was the flexible keel. The deck timbers were lightly attached to the ribs, which allowed the hull to be more flexible and give a little with the violent movement of Atlantic waves.

Above: Shipbuilders at work on a warship. (The picture is not to scale. In reality, the boat would have been bigger.)

Shipbuilding

Ships were made of oak or, where no oaks grew, pine. The keel was made first, and the stem and stern posts, each carved from one piece of wood, were attached. The hull was made of overlapping planks fastened with iron nails. It was made watertight with animal hair and tar. Curved parts were made from wood that was naturally curved, and wood was never cut against the grain (which can cause splitting). The shipbuilder's tools included a saw, hammer, ax, and adz (used for slicing a wooden surface).

Navigation

At sea, the Vikings navigated by the sun, stars, landmarks, and intelligent guesswork. They may have used an instrument called a sun compass that measured the height of the sun above the horizon, giving their latitude (distance north or south of the equator).

This 11th-century gilded (gold-coated) bronze weather vane from Norway probably once decorated the prow of a ship.

Viking ships were pointed at both ends. The sail was less useful when sailing into the wind.

Religion and Burials

Thor's hammer, which caused thunder when he threw it, was a common religious symbol. Like the Christian cross, it was often worn as a pendant.

Before they became Christians, the people of Scandinavia believed in a religion with many gods. Each god looked after one aspect of human life. For instance, Odin, the one-eyed chief, was god of war, wisdom, and poetry. He was wild and strange and rode an eight-legged horse. Two ravens brought him daily news of the world. Thor, Odin's son, after whom Thursday (Thor's Day) is named, was also warlike but was more down-to-earth and popular with ordinary people.

Religion

The old Norse religion had no holy book. It is not known exactly how people worshiped the gods, but it is known that they held feasts and made sacrifices of animals and sometimes even humans. Besides the gods, there were many other supernatural beings: the Norns, goddesses of Fate who held power over gods and humans; the Valkyries, warlike maidens who carried dead warriors to Valhalla; the crafty Loki and his son, the World Serpent; the wolf Fenrir; evil giants (Thor's great enemies); monsters; spirits; elves; and dwarves.

These figures from a medieval tapestry in a Swedish church represent the gods Odin (with battle-ax), Thor (with hammer), and Frey, god of fertility (with an ear of corn).

Burials

In Norse religion, when someone died, he was making a physical journey to the next world. So he was buried with many possessions for use in the afterlife, including horses and even servants. Important people were often buried in ships. The ships themselves were then buried under a mound or set on fire and pushed out to sea. Some graves were laid out with stones in the shape of a ship. The contents of graves have told us much about Viking life.

❶ SACRIFICED HORSE
❷ LOG BURIAL CHAMBER
❸ VIKING KING OR MASTER
❹ SACRIFICED SLAVE WOMAN
❺ SHIELD
❻ DEAD MAN'S HELMET AND WEAPONS
❼ DEAD MAN'S CHEST AND POSSESSIONS
❽ PAIL OF MILK OR WATER
❾ FUR BLANKET

The Oseberg ship

Archaeologists have discovered several ship burials. The richest, at Oseberg on Oslo Fjord, contained two female bodies, one probably a queen, the other a servant, who had died in 834. The tomb and its contents were well preserved. They included a beautiful cart (for the journey to the next world), five beds (ordinary people slept on the floor), and many wooden objects that, in other graves, have rotted away. These findings are more valuable to us than the lady's jewelry, which had been stolen!

This chief was buried with his servant girl and surrounded by grave goods that included his weapons, food and drink, and pottery.

In large ship burials, the body was usually placed in a wooden chamber, similar to a cabin, inside the ship. The ship here is modeled on the Oseberg funeral ship, which can be seen today in the Viking Ship Museum near Oslo.

A ninth-century picture stone from Gotland in Sweden. Here, Odin sits on his eight-legged horse Sleipnir, with Valkyries offering drinks. Besides their work as undertakers, the Valkyries acted as hostesses in Valhalla.

Valhalla

Odin, Lord of the Slain, lived in the vast, cold palace of Valhalla (Valhöll) in Asgard, home of the gods. The earls and warriors who had died in battle came to Valhalla. While they feasted, Odin sat apart, saying nothing and giving his food to his pet wolves. All awaited the last great battle, when the world would end at Ragnarök (Doomsday). Norse mythology contains hundreds of marvelous stories, which people probably treated as poetry.

Farming and Fishing

The Vikings are often thought of as seamen, voyagers, traders, and raiders, but their main occupation was farming. Nearly everything they needed was produced on the farm—not only food, but also clothing, furniture, tools, carts, and boats. The Vikings had to grow enough food to last through the long Scandinavian winter; when harvests were poor, people might starve. The whole family took part in working the farm, and slaves provided extra labor. Besides the usual farm work of tending crops and animals, many other jobs had to be done: brewing beer, cutting wood, and maintaining buildings, fences, tools, and boats.

Fish was preserved by drying or salting. It was caught by hook and line (in the winter, through holes in the ice), barbed spears (for salmon), or nets weighted with stones.

In spite of the hard work and, in some areas, difficult conditions, farmers in Scandinavia were doing well in the 8th to 10th centuries, and the population was rising.

Farming villages

Farms in Denmark often existed in groups of five or six farmsteads. They shared some services, such as a well or a blacksmith's workshop. Each farm had a longhouse, where both people and animals lived, and a few outbuildings. At long intervals, sometimes of 100 years or more, people left their village and built a new one close by.

Fishing

Most people lived near the sea, with its rich coastal fishing grounds, or close to lakes and rivers where large salmon ran. They ate a lot of fish, and in some areas, fishing was more important than farming. Hunting was another source of food. In addition to reindeer and elk, the Vikings in the far north hunted or trapped wild fowl, seals, and walruses (valuable for their skins, ivory, and oil) and collected shellfish and birds' eggs.

Farmers scattered seed by hand and used both horses and oxen as draft animals.

Farm crops

Only Denmark was warm enough to grow wheat. Elsewhere, the grain crops were barley (for beer and bread), oats (also used as winter feed for horses), and rye. Viking farmers grew vegetables, especially beans, peas, cabbage, onions, and hay for livestock. People collected wild plants, nuts, berries, and hops (for beer). In Hedeby, peach and plum trees grew. Since the Vikings drank mead, which is made with honey, they probably kept bees.

Farm animals

Viking farm animals were smaller than the animals on today's farms. The most valued were cattle and horses. Cattle provided milk, dairy products, and hides (leather), as well as meat. The Vikings also ate horse meat. Sheep produced wool for clothes. They were also sometimes used for milk and meat. Pigs and goats were widely kept, and poultry provided eggs, meat, and feathers for quilts.

Viking farmers used iron sheep shears and a wool comb to process wool.

Life on a Norwegian fjord was different from Denmark's fertile plain, but all over the Viking world, the typical home was a dark (windowless) and smoky longhouse.

Market towns

Most markets and towns were founded by kings or great chieftains. Hedeby was a small farming settlement until the Danish King Godfred made some merchants settle there in 808. Trade brought wealth, part of which came to the king in the form of taxes. As they grew, towns attracted people who wanted to escape life in the country.

Craftsmen made beads and ornaments. These glass fragments must have been recycled into beads, since glass was not made in Viking Scandinavia.

Traders carried their own weights in a cloth bag to weigh silver coins in the absence of a coin-based economy.

A large market town attracted merchants from all over Europe, including Arabs from Muslim Spain. It often resembled an international gathering, but it was also like a village, with the houses arranged in plots where families grew vegetables and kept a few animals.

Markets and Towns

At the beginning of the eighth century, Scandinavia was a land of small farming settlements. No real towns existed. However, the Scandinavians were already trading with neighbors in northwest Europe. A town such as Hedeby in Jutland began because it was a convenient center of trade, with easy links to both the Baltic and the North Seas. Merchants gathered there to buy and sell. At first, it was just a market, where few people lived year-round. Soon, workshops and services appeared to supply the local market and to produce or process goods for trade. The market became a town.

This small amber figure may have been used as a counter in a board game.

Ports

Markets were founded near the sea or on waterways close to it because the easiest way to transport goods, especially bulky goods such as timber or wine, was by boat. However, not all trade went by sea, and markets were sometimes held in the winter months when carts could travel more easily over the frozen ground.

Fur trade

Among the most valuable products supplied by Viking merchants were furs and animal skins. Swedish merchants settled on the east coast of the Baltic Sea and spread farther into Russia in search of costly sable and marten pelts. Some took payments in furs from local tribespeople, either by agreement or by force. Othere, a chief in northern Norway, told the English King Alfred (871–99) about the furs, feathers, and whalebone he received as tribute from the people he ruled in Lapland.

Right: Swedish traders buying and selling furs. At markets, people of different races and religions were more tolerant of each other.

Left: A glass beaker from an island near modern Birka. Expensive glassware of this kind was imported from the Rhineland region in Germany.

Exports

In general, Viking merchants exported raw materials such as furs and slaves in exchange for silver and luxuries. But Scandinavia had its own luxuries, including amber, which was (and still is) found around the shores of the Baltic Sea. Amber is the fossilized resin of a long-extinct fir tree (it sometimes contains trapped insects). A beautiful, clear, golden-reddish color, it is hard enough to be carved, polished, and used in jewelry.

Eastern Trade

Vikings became rich from both raids and trade. The Baltic region had many raw materials that southern Europe wanted, including furs, skins, timber, tar, amber, walrus ivory, and seal skins. Vikings traded all over Europe and beyond. Most trade was local, but their sailing skills also gave the Vikings control of long-distance trade routes. The greatest traders were the Swedes, who crossed the Baltic and traveled through Russia and central Europe, finally reaching Byzantium. They traded raw materials and slaves for Eastern silver and luxury goods such as spices, silks, and jewelry.

The trade routes covered great distances. The ships that followed the coastal routes were broader and deeper than Viking warships, with fewer oars. They could take 44 to 55 tons (40-50 t) of cargo.

Trade routes

The Vikings were traders before they became raiders. They had trading posts throughout northern Europe. By the 11th century, their trade routes stretched from Greenland in the west to Southwest Asia in the east, although traffic was light on distant routes. Wherever possible, they traveled by water to cross Russia, using boats that could be carried when necessary.

One group of Vikings attacked Constantinople in 860, but trade was more profitable than war in the Byzantine Empire.

Constantinople

When the first small Russian state, known as Rus, was founded in the ninth century, Swedish Vikings were involved. They were called "Rus," and along with the native Slavs, they helped to develop the large trading towns of Novgorod and Kiev, rivals as capital of Rus. From there, Swedish traders moved deeper into Russia until they reached their goal, Constantinople, capital of the Byzantine empire and the greatest, wealthiest city in Europe.

Exotic treasure

The goods that Viking merchants wanted to buy were mainly luxuries that did not exist in Scandinavia, such as wine from southern Europe or rare silks from the East. In Viking graves, archaeologists have discovered surprising objects that came from lands never even visited by the Vikings. They must have been bought and sold many times before they reached Scandinavia.

One of the strangest treasures of the Vikings is this small, sixth-century figure of Buddha, found in Sweden but made 5,000 miles (8,000 km) away in northern India.

The Varangian Guard

The reputation of the Vikings as great warriors was known in the East, and the Byzantine emperor hired them as his personal guards. Known as Varangians, they served as Byzantium's finest regiment from the 9th to 11th centuries. Among them was Harald Hardrada, future king of Norway, whose defeat by Harold of England in 1066 marked the end of the Viking age.

Right: A Byzantine mosaic that shows a soldier of the Varangian Guard.

Arab traders may have sold this bronze brazier, or portable stove, to Swedes. It is Islamic in style and was made in Baghdad in the ninth century.

To Vikings, the value of silver coins lay in their weight. Coins were cut up to make the right weight, and silver objects such as rings were used in the same way.

Viking traders arriving in Constantinople. They could travel from their bases in northwest Russia almost entirely by water: down the River Dnieper and across the Black Sea. It was a shorter and easier route than sailing via the Mediterranean.

Houses and Homes

The people of the Viking age were not great builders. It appears that the only large buildings before the stave, or wooden, churches of Christian times were in a few royal forts, such as Trelleborg in Jutland, where large chieftain's houses were found. Houses varied regionally, and people used the materials available locally, usually wood, but in Iceland, where wood was scarce, houses were made of turf on a stone base. Houses were built to last a generation or so. Today, little trace of them remains.

This German wine jug (used to transport wine) and lidded drinking pot are the work of skilled craftsmen. They must have belonged to rich families, because most vessels were homemade.

Houses might be wood, stone, or turf. Walls were often made of wattle and daub (thin willow branches woven into a framework and covered with mud) supported between wooden uprights. Roofs were wooden, thatched, or turf.

The longhouse

The roof of a house was built on horizontal beams supported by two rows of posts running the length of the building. Therefore, it could be as long as necessary (some were more than 160 feet, or 50 m, long) but only about 16 feet (5 m) wide. It was divided into two parts, one for people, the other for storage and winter stables for animals. People lived, ate, and slept in one big room.

Archaeologists have found evidence that some furniture, such as chests and stools, existed in Viking houses.

In a rich household, slaves might do the cooking. Most houses had a cauldron hanging from an iron tripod over the fire.

Around the hearth

Families gathered around the hearth for meals and stories, which were the main forms of entertainment on long winter evenings. With no windows, the house was dark and smoky. The only furniture was a few chests, and most people slept on the low platforms along the walls. An important man might have a special chair and a proper bed. In the towns, houses were smaller. Craftsmen's houses contained a workshop in addition to the living room.

Food and cooking

The center of the house was the hearth, where an open fire burned. Food was cooked in iron, clay, or soapstone pots and eaten off wooden plates. Some settlements shared a bread oven. People ate two meals a day, and their diet was healthy, with plenty of meat and fish, fresh fruit, and vegetables. Many foods could be dried for the winter.

Most houses contained a loom. This whalebone plaque, decorated with heads of fantastic creatures, may have been for smoothing the woven cloth.

Under lock and key

Valuable possessions, such as jewelry, silver, and perhaps weapons, were kept locked up inside a chest. Scandinavian locksmiths made excellent locks, which usually worked with a key that squeezed or released springs inside the lock.

Archaeologists have often found keys in women's graves, which suggests that the wife was responsible for the household keys.

❶ UPRIGHT LOOM

❷ SMOKE HOLE

❸ THATCHED ROOF

❹ DRIED MEATS AND FISH HANG FROM THE RAFTERS

❺ HEARTH

❻ CAULDRON FOR COOKING

❼ COOKING UTENSILS AND CONTAINERS

❽ THE EARTHEN FLOOR WAS OFTEN COVERED IN REEDS AND GRASS

The Överhogdal tapestry from Sweden depicts animals, both real and imaginary. The original would have hung on a wall. This is a modern copy made by the same methods.

Making clothes

In a Viking family, the mother ran the household and looked after the children. She had far more duties than a modern housewife, because on farming homesteads, families made their own food, clothes, and other necessities. Food came from their own animals and crops, and clothes were made of wool from their own sheep. A few items, such as iron tools, were bought from traveling salesmen or town markets.

In spinning, fibers were attached to a wooden stick called a spindle (right) by pulling them from a mass of wool held on a distaff. As the weighted spindle dropped, it spun, twisting the fiber into thread.

Viking tapestry

Cloth soon rots, and only a few scraps have survived from the Viking period. Besides clothing, people made tapestries (on a loom) and embroidery (done with a needle) to decorate the houses of the rich. Small pieces from a strip of tapestry, showing a procession of horses, carts, and people, were found in the famous ship burial at Oseberg in 1904.

Women spinning (above) and carding the fleece (separating it into fibers, left). There are many different steps involved in producing cloth from raw wool. One is weaving the thread into cloth. Viking women used an upright loom, which sometimes stood against a wall. The vertical threads (the warp) were kept tight by weights at the bottom. The horizontal threads (the weft) were then woven by hand.

Clothing and Jewelry

The victims of the Vikings' raids saw them as wild men—violent and frightening bandits with rough beards and uncombed hair. Viking raiders were certainly violent, but that is only a small part of the Viking story. Rich families were well dressed and wore expensive jewelry. Poorer people, who could not afford ornaments, dressed differently but still took pride in how they looked. Men might have long hair and were well-groomed, with trimmed mustaches and beards. Different regions had different styles of dress, and there were various fashions throughout the Viking Age.

Right: This Viking man wears outdoor clothes, with a fur-trimmed hat.

Clothing

Scandinavian winters are cold, and people needed to dress warmly. Men wore long pants or breeches. On top, men generally wore a tunic under a cloak. Women wore an underdress with a tunic, fastened with brooches at the shoulders. Outdoors, both men and women wore a heavy cloak. Men's cloaks were fastened at the left shoulder by a brooch. Leather and fur were also worn. The clothes of wealthy people were often decorated with embroidery or edged with fur.

Shoes could be made from one piece of leather stitched together over the foot. Men also wore tough boots that rose to the ankle or higher.

Among the objects found most often in Viking graves are glass beads. This necklace also contains other materials—rock crystal, metals, and colored stones.

This silver, patterned arm ring was found in Denmark.

Jewelry

Like other early peoples of Europe, the Scandinavians liked personal display, and if they could afford it, they wore a lot of silver jewelry. You could judge the importance of a person by the jewelry he or she wore. A rich man's solid gold neck ring could weigh more than two pounds (1 kg), and in an emergency, it could be used as money. Jewelers also worked with many other, cheaper materials, such as copper, bronze, glass, amber, jet, and red cornelian.

This brooch is decorated with enamel and precious stones.

Hairstyles

Other Viking objects that archaeologists often find are combs. Both men and women had long hair, and they liked it neat. Combing also removed head lice. Men wore their hair loose or rolled on the neck (like the man at right). Some women had elaborate hairstyles that formed a complicated knot.

This head, carved from elk antler, shows the neatly kept beard and mustache of a Viking warrior. There is something unusual about this cheerful Swede—smiling faces are rare in Viking art.

Children and Growing Up

Childhood was very short in Viking times, and children had to grow up quickly. The Danish King Cnut was only 18 years old when he took command of the army. Girls were usually married at the age of 15. A family household typically included parents, grandparents, children, perhaps other relations, and slaves. Several different types of toys have been found by archaeologists. Many of these toys—such as horses, boats, and swords—reflected adult life. In addition to playing with toys, Viking children also practiced many sports, including swimming and ball games.

Toys such as this wooden horse were made for Viking children.

This wooden cup (left) was made to be held by an adult feeding an infant (or an invalid). The baby's chair (below) has a crossbar to prevent the child from falling out.

Infants

Before modern medicines, life was especially dangerous for young people, and many died as babies or small children. Parents might leave an unwanted baby out in the wild to die, and poor parents sometimes sold their children as slaves. Young children, mainly boys, might go to live with relatives, thus gaining two sets of parents.

Education

The Vikings had no schools or universities. Parents and other family members taught children everything they needed to know. Boys learned how to grow crops and care for livestock, how to build a house and sail a ship, how to hunt and fish, and how to fight. Girls learned the household crafts, especially cooking and the many skills needed to make clothing. Girls also had to know how to look after the farm.

Viking boys learned the skills they needed to be successful farmers and warriors.

Storytelling

The Vikings had no films, televisions, computers, or even books. Their main entertainment was storytelling. In important households, a professional storyteller entertained everyone, but every family told its own stories as well. Family history, handed down in this way, was important to the Vikings. Yet surnames as we understand them did not exist. A boy was named after his father—Leif Ericsson means Leif, son of Eric.

Left: A kind of recorder made of bone, which may have been played by children in Sweden. Above: Someone in the Faroe Islands made this simple wooden model of a boat for a child.

Toys and games

We know little about children in Viking times. Few children's graves, and no rune stones (memorials), have been found. However, archaeologists have dug up many toys, including carved wooden models of animals, boats, tools, and swords. Board games and dice, which adults probably played as well, have also been found. There are also stories about game-playing, and in some wooden carvings, people seem to be playing a game.

An old lady tells a story to her grandchildren. Like the stories in the Sagas (see page 42), it might be about gods and magic or famous heroes, perhaps their own ancestors.

This gold foil from Norway shows a man and woman embracing.

Marriage

Marriages were usually arranged between the families of the bridegroom and the bride. Men and women played different roles in Viking society and appear in many ways to have been equal partners in marriage. A woman often ran the household or farm when her husband was away. Arab travelers were amazed that women had the right to divorce and could inherit property.

Entertainment

Some Viking men led active and often violent lives, but it was not all farming, fighting, and feasting. Some men were craftsmen who did not go on raids or fight with their neighbors. Nearly everyone enjoyed music, stories, riddles, and games that required brains rather than muscles. A warrior had to be both clever and strong—to speak as well as he fought. Jugglers, acrobats, and traveling minstrels performed at fairs and markets. Some Viking sports were peaceful, although they were often connected with hunting or fighting.

Men gambled with dice like these, usually made of animal bone or horn. Some were not square, but oblong.

Viking sports

People seldom played sports just for amusement. Sports had other, more serious purposes, usually connected with skill in battle or obtaining meat. In Norway, the winner of an archery contest received a prize. Ball games were also played.

Music

Although full-time musicians worked in the households of the rich, ordinary people sang songs and made their own music. Unfortunately, we do not know what this music sounded like. Bone pipes, similar to recorders (see page 29), have been found in settlements, along with other types of instruments, including an early kind of harp, lyres, horns, wooden pipes, and drums.

These 10th-century boxwood panpipes were found in York in northern England.

The Vikings enjoyed physical contests and tests of strength and skill. They even staged duels between horses, to which they attached horns. An argument over the result might end with the owners of the horses fighting each other. Wrestling was mainly a lower-class sport and often ended in serious injury.

The Vikings enjoyed playing board games, especially during the winter months.

There was plenty of eating and drinking at Viking feasts.

Games

We know the names of several board games played in Scandinavia and in Viking settlements, although we do not know the rules. Their names usually end in "tafl," meaning table or board, and they may have been different versions of the same game. Archaeologists have found several types of boards and counters. The most common games were for "hnefatafl," a kind of war game that included a king and soldiers. The boards were divided into small squares, sometimes with small holes for pegged pieces.

The Vikings may have learned chess from Arab traders. These 12th-century chess pieces come from the Hebrides.

Right: Drinking cups were made from small horns. Vikings had to finish the drink in one gulp, since the cups had no flat base and could not be put down.

Feasting

Feasts could bring people together and strengthen the loyalties of families and clans. Important chiefs held feasts for their followers. News was exchanged, weddings were arranged, bargains were made, and feuds were started. Feasts could be rowdy, since Vikings drank a lot, but they also included music, dancing, and storytelling. Everyone feasted at the three main festivals—spring, harvest, and midwinter.

Hunting

Hunting with horses, hounds, and falconry (tame hawks) has always been the sport of kings and noblemen. However, most Vikings used bows and arrows or spears to kill animals ranging from walruses to hares. In parts of Norway, fishing was a way of life—iron hooks and barbed salmon spears have been found.

This 11th-century scene from the Bayeux Tapestry shows a sportsman hunting with hounds and a falcon.

Viking Fortifications

Defensive camps and fortifications are the largest structures to have been built in the Viking age. Early fortifications were temporary and were used as refuges by people from the surrounding countryside in times of war. A few Scandinavian settlements, such as Hedeby and Birka, were also fortified with large, semi-circular structures. Archaeologists have also found five large, circular settlements, usually called royal fortresses. They date from the late 10th century.

❶ VIKING SOLDIERS ON GUARD

❷ FORTIFIED WALLS

❸ WATCHTOWER

❹ TIMBER FOOTPATHS

❺ HOUSES AND WORKSHOPS: BLACKSMITHS AND JEWELERS ALSO WORKED INSIDE THE FORTIFICATIONS

❻ RIVER RUNNING THROUGH THE STREETS

❼ MANY WOMEN AND CHILDREN LIVED INSIDE THE FORTIFICATIONS

Fyrkat

Of the five fortresses, archaeologists have studied Fyrkat, in northeast Jutland, most closely. It consists of four groups of buildings arranged in squares. The buildings are similar to extra-large longhouses, but they have curved side walls, with supporting buttresses on all four sides. They were built of oak, and the two streets that divide them into groups were laid with timber planks. Wooden boards also lined the outer ramparts, making them harder for attackers to climb if they made it across the moat.

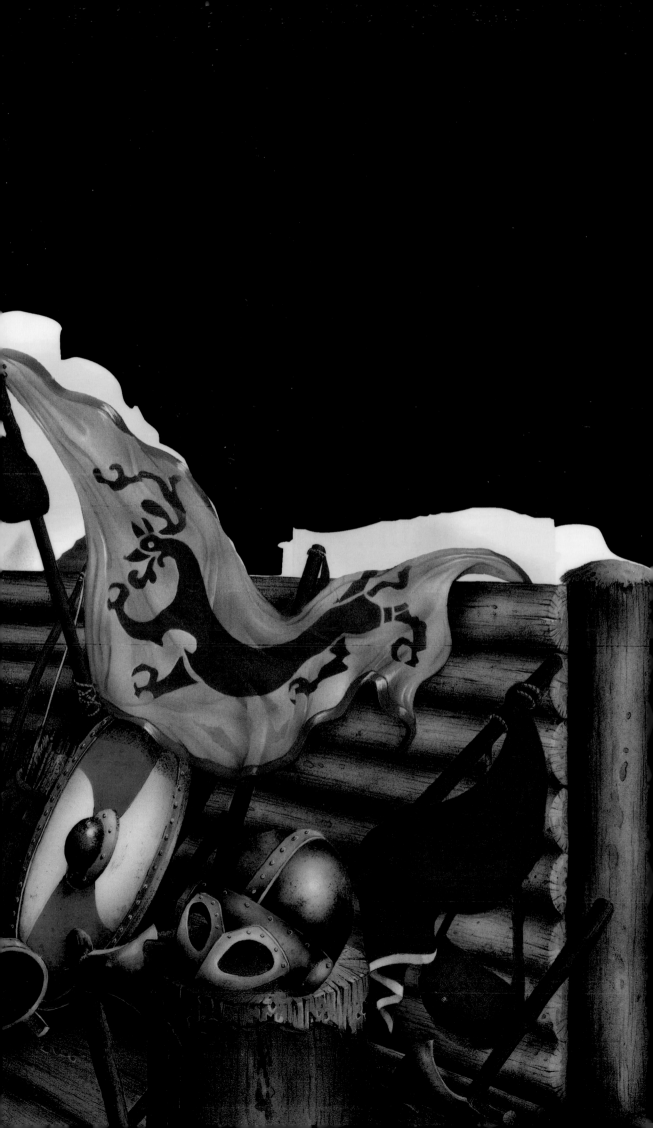

An artist's reconstruction of Fyrkat. The fortresses (unknown before 1940) could only have been built by a powerful central government, perhaps a royal government.

Barracks or capital?

The five fortresses are so alike that they must have been based on the same plan and built at roughly the same time. When first discovered, their regular plan made experts think they were military barracks—places for gathering troops (perhaps for a planned invasion of England). Then archaeologists discovered women and children buried in the graveyards, as well as barns and craftsmen's workshops among the buildings. So ordinary people must have lived there, too. More than just barracks, the fortresses were probably regional centers of royal government for enforcing peace and justice and collecting taxes.

Construction work

The Danish fortresses required skillful planning, much labor, and great expense. At Fyrkat, construction of the rampart required the shifting of about 350,000 cubic feet (10,000 cu m) of earth. Thousands of oak trees were cut down for the buildings, roads, and fences. The towns of Hedeby (below) and Birka were dominated by large citadels, and the surrounding walls were interspersed with huge watchtowers.

Many workers (perhaps slaves) were needed to cut down the trees, make them into planks of the right size, carry them to the building site, and erect the buildings.

The massive semi-circular rampart surrounding the market town of Hedeby in Jutland (see pages 20–21) was more than 4,265 feet (1,300 m) long and, in places, stood as high as 33 feet (10 m). Inside the fortified walls was a bustling community and trading center with wattle and daub houses that served as dwellings, workshops, and stores. Hedeby's streets were paved with timber-planked footpaths, and a small river ran through its streets.

The Viking Raids

The Vikings first appeared on European coasts as savage raiders in the 790s. In their swift longships, they arrived without warning and attacked undefended villages and monasteries. They killed unarmed people without mercy, carried off prisoners to sell as slaves, and seized everything valuable they could carry. At first, the raids lasted only a few days in the summer. Later, large armies arrived and stayed through the winter. Finally, the invaders began to settle as colonists.

Danes conquered nearly all of the English kingdoms until King Alfred of Wessex defeated Guthrum at Edington and agreed to divide the country in 878.

This Scandinavian helmet was made before Viking times. Viking helmets were rare and usually took the form of a simple iron cap.

In the Viking raid on Lindisfarne (Holy Island) in northern England in 793, the church was looted. Many monks were killed or drowned, and some religious relics were destroyed.

Berserkers

Berserkers (bear-shirts) were a special class of warriors who wore animal skins. They attacked their enemy, screaming and yelling in a crazy lust for blood. Disciples of the war god, Odin, are said to have had no fear and felt no pain. Only death stopped them. Although they were great warriors, Viking leaders distrusted berserkers because they could not control them.

It was said that berserkers, in their murderous rage, would bite their own shields. This berserker (right) comes from the Lewis chess set (see page 31).

The warrior

The more prominent Viking raiders were bands of men led by their chief. Fighting was their business, and they would follow their chief to the death. They fought on foot, man-to-man. When the small groups of raiders became whole armies, they included ordinary farmers who were not as well armed. Some may have had only an ax from their farm, but they were all fierce fighters.

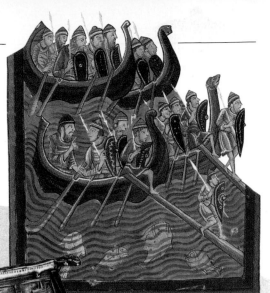

The warrior's chief weapons were swords, spears, and battle-axes. For defense, warriors carried round, wooden shields and occasionally wore dome-shaped helmets.

The raids begin

The first known Viking raid occurred in 793. Vikings attacked the English abbey of Lindisfarne on an island off Northumbria in northern England. It was an easy target, since monasteries were often built in exposed, remote places. The terrified monks had never expected danger from the sea. Monasteries and churches made attractive victims. They were undefended and contained gold and silver objects, among other treasures.

Right: This painting from a 12th-century book shows a Danish army approaching the English coast. The English called their attackers Danes, but they also included Norwegians and others.

This jeweled, bronze casket was found in Norway, but it came from a Scottish abbey or church and would have held relics (such as bones) of a Christian saint.

Targets

The Vikings' first overseas raids were violent robberies. The raids were small and unorganized, however. When larger and more frequent attacks began on the mainland of Europe, the main targets were not remote monasteries, but trading centers and large towns. Such raids began in the 830s, when the empire of Charlemagne (died 814), which was once well defended, was breaking up.

This memorial stone from Lindisfarne shows charging Viking raiders. It was carved not long after the attack.

The Vikings in France

By 840, the strong Frankish empire of Charlemagne had disappeared. The Frankish lands were divided between three quarrelsome brothers. Loyalty and honor disappeared as local lords followed their own selfish interests. This allowed the Vikings to raid towns far inland. In the 840s, they sailed up the Loire and Seine Rivers. Hundreds were slaughtered in the capture of Rouen in 841 and Nantes in 843. In 845, 120 Danish ships reached Paris. They returned several times looking for somewhere to settle. In 911, the French king offered land around the lower Seine to Vikings led by Rollo. Their descendants were called Normans, and their land was known as Normandy.

This illustration from a French manuscript shows Viking soldiers on their way up the Loire to attack Angers. In real life, they would have been yelling threats and waving their swords!

Up the Seine

The region of the Seine became the Vikings' favorite hunting ground. When Ragnar and his Danes sacked Paris in 845, they enjoyed themselves so much that they refused to leave until the king paid them 7,000 pounds (3,175 kg) of silver. Other rulers, such as King Ethelred of England, were also forced to pay the Vikings a ransom to get rid of them. Unfortunately, this did not prevent them from coming back the next year!

The Vikings used bows and arrows, stones, and blazing boats to attack the Île de la Cité.

The Viking longships, which sailed across deep oceans, could also sail up a shallow creek.

The Vikings preferred to fight hand-to-hand and used bows and arrows mainly for hunting. The bow, however, was a useful weapon in a siege, since arrows could be shot over walls.

Viking destruction

By 850, the Vikings were using European rivers almost as freely as people today use highways. France was in chaos. The old government had broken down. Any man of wealth could build a private castle and hire others to serve him as soldiers in exchange for his protection. Meanwhile, Viking pirates sailed around Spain and into the Mediterranean. In 885, they launched their largest attack yet on Paris.

Paris besieged

The Franks tried to stop the Viking invasions by building fortified bridges across the rivers. There were two on the Seine at Paris. The Viking force that reached them in 885 was enormous. It was said that there were 700 ships, and they were prepared to wait. The people in the city held out for a year until the French king arrived with an army. He persuaded the Vikings to leave peacefully, giving them supplies and silver in return.

Paris was not a large city like Rome. Citizens could take shelter within city walls on an island in the Seine. When the Vikings tried to climb the walls, the Parisians poured hot tar on them.

This memorial stone (right) from the island of Gotland, off Sweden, shows warriors with shields and swords. Touching swords was a way of swearing loyalty and support.

The end of the raids

The rulers of Christian Europe finally found a way to stop the destruction of Viking raids. Since Vikings restlessly sought good land, groups such as Rollo's band agreed that if offered land, they would guard the country against other raiders. In time, the Scandinavian settlers mixed with the local people and forgot their Viking ancestry.

Iceland

Iceland once had more trees than it has today. The Viking pioneers settled mainly along the temperate coastline, including near the present capital of Reykjavik, but most of Iceland was covered in ice or volcanic lava. Since wood was scarce, families built their houses out of stone and turf. Iceland had some advantages, however, including hot springs. In freezing weather, people could enjoy a warm outdoor bath!

Above: Cutting up a whale. Whales were often stranded on North Atlantic coasts, but Icelanders also hunted them with harpoons.

Greenland

In 982, Eric the Red left Iceland on a three-year voyage to explore the coasts of Greenland. When he returned, he persuaded people to settle there, calling it "Greenland," to make it sound attractive. In 985, 25 ships followed him to Eric's Fjord (only 14 arrived) to find good grassland, fresh water, and even small trees. The sea was full of fish and the land full of animals. Soon, more families arrived, and their descendants lived in Greenland for 400 years.

Greenlanders stayed in touch with Europe for a long time, wearing European fashions, such as this hooded cape from the 14th century.

Discovering North America

Upon hearing of land to the west, Leif Ericsson explored the coast as far as a place he called "Vinland" (wine-land) because grapes or berries grew there. His men built houses in which they stayed all winter. Others followed, but because of fighting with local people, the colony only lasted three years. Recently, Norwegian experts found remains of such a Viking settlement at L'Anse aux Meadows in Newfoundland.

Left: A soapstone whorl—a weight that keeps the spindle turning when spinning fiber into yarn. Found at L'Anse aux Meadows, it must have belonged to Europeans.

Arrival in the West

Some of the people who left their homes in the ninth century to seek more land or to escape the growing power of kings settled in lands across the North Atlantic, beginning with the Shetland Islands and, in about 860, the Faroe Islands. Vikings, mostly Norwegians, then began to settle in large numbers in present-day Iceland, which was largely uninhabited. About 100 years later, Eric the Red discovered good pastures along the fjords of southwest Greenland and led colonists there in 985. In about 1000, his son, Leif Ericsson, became the first European to land in North America.

This wooden figure of a Norse trader was made by Inuits (Eskimos) in northern Greenland in about 1400.

Above: The western settlements. Norse colonies in Iceland began in the 870s. Eric the Red found eastern Greenland icebound but discovered grassy fjords (similar to those in Iceland and Norway) in the southwest. Leif Ericsson discovered "Vinland," probably Newfoundland.

Pioneers

To make a home in a land where no one lived, the Norse settlers had to work fast and adapt to new conditions. For example, the roof of Eric's house in Greenland had rafters made of whale's ribs, since no large trees grew there. The Greenlanders also discovered a simple way of fishing by digging a trench near the water's edge at low tide. The tide came in, bringing halibut, which were trapped in the trench when the tide went out again.

Sailing from Iceland to Greenland took four days or longer, and settlers had to carry food and supplies. When they arrived, they worked fast, building a turf house in a few days. Food, especially meat and fish, was abundant, but for some goods, they depended on imports from Iceland.

Christianization

The Vikings were pagans who worshiped many different gods. They thought nothing of killing Christian priests or destroying monasteries, but growing contacts with the organized, Christian kingdoms of Europe brought changes. To the Christian Church, the pagan north was a challenge. Missionaries and others tried to convert the northerners. Some Viking merchants found trading easier if they became Christians, as did groups who settled in Christian countries. The spread of Christianity in Scandinavia also coincided with the creation of strong monarchies.

This little, silver crucifix comes from a 10th-century grave at Birka in Sweden. It is one of the oldest Christian symbols found in Scandinavia and, judging by the style, must have been made there.

This scene appears on a gilded silver plate from a church in Jutland, Denmark. The design is embossed, hammered out from the back, and shows the baptism (in about 965) of Harald Bluetooth, king of Denmark.

Spread of Christianity

As had happened in other countries, kings realized that partnership with the Christian Church strengthened royal rule. But their power was limited. When Hakon, a Christian, became king of Norway in 935, he called in English missionaries to help make his people Christians. He failed, although Christianity did gain a foothold. Olaf Tryggvason forced his subjects to convert, but they returned to the Norse religion after his death in 1000. Christianity was finally established during the reign of Harald Olafsson (1015–30).

This decorated rune stone at Jelling, Denmark, was erected by the powerful Harald Bluetooth (reigned about 958–87), who is said to have converted the Danes to Christianity.

Conversion to Christianity

Change came more quickly in Viking settlements abroad. Danes invading East Anglia killed its Christian king, Edmund, in 870. They settled in the region, and 30 years later, they were making memorials to Edmund the Martyr. For some time, Christian and pagan beliefs existed side by side. Helgi the Skinny, an Iceland colonist, believed in Christ, but when in danger, he prayed to Thor. Eric the Red, who founded the Greenland colony, refused to accept Christianity, but his wife Thjodhild accepted it and locked him out of their bedroom!

Above: This tapestry from 12th-century Sweden shows Christian bell-ringers at work. Their purpose was to frighten off the monsters that belonged to Norse mythology.

The basic plan of a stave church was a square with four tall, strong, upright posts at the corners. It became larger and more elaborate as time went on, but the basic design remained a series of squares. In the final version (after the Viking age), the whole building was raised above the ground to prevent it from rotting.

Stave churches

After Scandinavia became Christian, many churches were built. They were quite different from the churches being built in older Christian lands. These magnificent churches were made of wood. They were built, like a ship, from wooden planks or staves (the boards that make up a barrel) and are known as stave churches. The walls were made of upright timbers held together by horizontal beams at the top and bottom. They were most common in Norway. One or two still survive today.

Christian crafts

One way to measure the growing influence of Christianity in Scandinavia is by the number of Christian objects found in graves (even though, as Christianity took hold, grave goods became less common). The most common are religious ornaments in the form of small crosses. Up to the 11th century or later, they were usually made in the same artistic style as symbols of the Norse religion, such as Thor's hammers.

An 11th-century gilded copper figure of Christ crucified. It comes from an early Christian church in Jutland.

❶ SHINGLED, WOODEN ROOF

❷ DRAGON HEAD DECORATIONS

❸ VIKING CONGREGATION: MANY VIKING PEOPLE STOOD DURING THE RELIGIOUS CEREMONY

❹ CARVED, WOODEN BENCHES

❺ THE MOST IMPORTANT PEOPLE IN VIKING SOCIETY SAT IN CARVED, WOODEN CHAIRS AT THE FRONT OF THE CHURCH

❻ BAPTISMAL FONT

Writing and Literature

The different Scandinavian peoples all spoke forms of the same language. Few people could read until Christian times, and there were no books. The stories found in the Icelandic sagas were passed on by word of mouth, some for centuries, before they were written down. However, the Vikings did have a form of written letters, called runes, which we know mostly from memorial stones, or rune stones. Runic writing was more common in towns, where people used it for purposes such as record keeping.

The large Rök stone in Sweden (above), covered in writing, is a man's memorial to his dead son. Many rune stones had pictures, such as this mask from Denmark (right), carved and then painted in bright colors.

Runes were made up of vertical or sloping lines. They had no horizontal lines, because if carved on wood, they became confused with the grain of the wood.

The Viking alphabet

The "futhark," or alphabet, had only 16 letters. The same letter could stand for different sounds, and some sounds had no letter: "o" or "e" had none, but "a" had two. As a result, a word might be spelled in different ways, which makes runic writing very hard to read. It was not suitable for long texts. The Rök stone is the longest inscription that has survived.

Rune stones

Some families put up memorials in the form of carved stone slabs to remember a famous relative or perhaps to record a journey. They were usually placed in prominent places such as crossroads or river fords. Most of the runic writing that has lasted comes from these rune stones, but people also wrote on other materials such as bone and wood.

Literature

The Icelandic sagas are one of the great treasures of European literature. They were written in the 12th to 13th centuries, although they were previously recited by skalds (poets) and recorded only in memory. Some of the sagas are fiction stories of vivid fantasy. Other sagas describe the deeds of dead kings and heroes of legend. A few, such as Egil's Saga, tell of more ordinary people.

Poetry

Some of the sagas are in prose, but most are poems, which were easier to memorize. Poets called skalds recited them at the courts of nobles, and skaldic poetry tells of the great deeds of their patrons. Another form, known as Eddic poetry, tells the stories of Norse gods and heroes.

A picture of Egil Skallagrimsson—warrior, trader, poet, and farmer—the hero of Egil's Saga. It comes from a manuscript written after the Viking age.

Left: A 13th-century illustration from the "Flateyjarbok," a 226-page collection of sagas. It includes the Greenland Saga, describing Leif Ericsson's discovery of North America. Also depicted here is the Norwegian king Olaf Tryggvason killing a boar and a sea-ogress.

Since runes had to be cut with a knife or chisel, they were formed from straight lines only. Cutting a curve is much more difficult, especially in stone.

Rune stones were carved and decorated by special craftsmen. The runes were often painted red, black, or white.

Carving the rune stones

There was an air of magic about runes. The Vikings believed that Odin, the god of poetry and war, had invented them. In early times, they were used as magic charms, which were written on weapons to protect the warrior. Memorial stones came later. Sometimes, a man made his own memorial. An inscription at Väsby reads: "Ali had this stone put up in his own honor."

Inside the workshop

The blacksmith's workshop contained a
furnace, where the metal was heated until
soft, and an anvil, on which the metal was
shaped with hammers and other tools.
Tools have been found buried in graves
with their owners.
Blacksmiths were
important and
highly respected
figures in Viking
society. Their skills
seemed almost
magical, and they
appear in several myths
and legends.

*The most popular of
Scandinavian pagan
gods, Thor, was
commonly portrayed
as a blacksmith with
his hammer and anvil.*

*Oval brooches such as
these (left) were made
in clay molds by
special craftsmen.
Cheap brooches were
mass-produced for less
wealthy Vikings.*

*The blacksmith's workshop was
usually found on the edge of Viking
towns because of the risk of fire. Blacksmiths
produced everything from weapons and tools to
domestic items such as pots and pans.*

Metalwork

A farmer depends on his tools—a warrior on his weapons. Viking craftsmen were highly skilled, and their metalwork was among the best in Europe. Iron was used for weapons and tools and in the construction of boats and ships. The iron ore was found mainly in bogs and lakes. It was smelted with charcoal into raw iron in special furnaces, then hammered into bars and transported to the blacksmith's forge. There, it was reheated and shaped into objects. Metalworkers also used other metals, such as bronze and lead, which could be cast in a mold.

A Viking sword hilt, which may have been used in ceremonies as well as battles.

Right: This type of dress pin, made of gilded bronze, was used for fastening a cloak at the shoulder.

Everyday objects

A large number of useful and decorative objects—ranging from gold and silver jewelry to bronze fittings for horse harnesses to iron nails, boat rivets, and needles—were made of metal. The cauldron, or kettle, that hung over the hearth was made of iron sheets riveted together. Many tools were made of metal. Even wooden tools such as spades often had an iron edge.

Below: Tongs once used by a Scandinavian blacksmith to hold hot metal as it was shaped.

Weaponsmiths

Sword blades, knives, axes, spears, and arrowheads were made of iron. A good sword was valuable, and the methods of the swordsmiths were very advanced. The two cutting edges of a sword blade were made of the hardest metal. The center was composed of plaited strips for greater flexibility and a striking appearance.

In 1936, archaeologists made this amazing find in a bog on the island of Gotland, Sweden. The tool chest contained about 200 types of tools for both wood and metalwork. They may have belonged to a rich household or a shipyard.

The metalworker's tools

One important product of the blacksmith's forge, or workshop, was the tools. Because many settlements, especially in Norway, were isolated, each one had a blacksmith's forge, and ordinary farmers may have made and repaired their own iron tools. The finest work, such as the gold and silver sword hilt above, was done by full-time craftsmen, often in towns.

Index